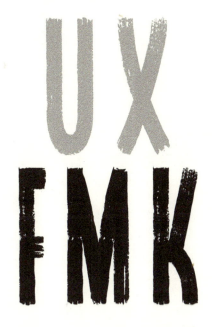

USER EXPERIENCE:
F**K, MARRY, OR KILL

TIM BROADWATER

TABLE OF CONTENTS

🧪 ATTENTION

✂ 20 F**KS TO GIVE

⏰ 20 Lessons in Marriage

ATTENTION

A SPECIAL NOTE ABOUT HOW THIS BOOK WAS CREATED

Dear User Experience professional, thank you for claiming your copy of *UX: FMK (User Experience: F**k, Marry, or Kill)*. This book will teach you critical User Experience skills, tools, and techniques that every User Experience professional needs to understand and apply. This book was originally created as a live interview. That's why it reads as a conversation rather than a traditional "book" that talks "at" you. I wanted you to feel as though I am talking with you, much like a close friend or relative. I felt that creating the material this way would make it easier for you to grasp the topics and put them to use quickly, rather than wading through hundreds of pages.

So, relax. Grab a highlighter, pen or pencil, and some paper to take notes. And get ready to take your User Experience to the next level so that you can understand how to succeed in the field of User Experience despite the feeling that everything always seems to change.

Let's get started with *UX: FMK...*

Yours,

Tim Broadwater

FOREWORD

User Experience (UX) design has exploded over the past two to three decades. Being in the design industry for nearly four decades, I have witnessed the evolution and convergence of Design Thinking as we recognize it today. I have worked in a host of creative design settings, from small to mid-sized studios to enormous Fortune 500 corporate office environments, eventually owning my own studio. As an academician, I have worked at five institutions of higher learning, having authored and chaired a graduate-level UX Master of Arts program. These experiences provide me a unique insight to the creative process from the designer's perspective, but also the cognitive reception from the user's perspective.

Even though there exists a myriad of Design Thinking flavors today, the core structure remains consistent. Long gone are the days in which design studios work directly with clients in a silo and omit the end user. In this day and age, it's actually hard to believe omitting the end user was the design process of that time. Current UX design processes provide "design intelligence", as UX professionals (UXers) today are much more understanding, informed, and prepared when they start the brainstorming and ideation phases. UXers are far better equipped to render successful design solutions because of the research and analysis that happens before they put the proverbial "pen to paper."

Tim's Broadwater's UX: FMK (User Experience: F**K, Marry, or Kill) looks at the UX design process with a fresh attitude from a contemporary UXer's point of view. In many academic settings, we have adopted and been inundated with the same established books from the development era of UX. As these transition into a more historical context in terms of how we arrived to the point where we are today, Broadwater's text addresses the modern process(es) and experiences UX designers face today, with all of the joys, challenges, and frustrations they entail. To get the most out of Design Thinking and UX, you must be faithful to the process. Many times, this requires additional time, attention, and expense. Broadwater guides you through the experience in a modern vibe and lays out, in plain terms, the theories and principles that lead to success.

David Edwin Meyers, MFA

Professor of Interactive Design and Game Development,
Savannah College of Art and Design

INTRODUCTION

Well, I started out 20+ years ago as an art teacher and I couldn't get a job that was full time. I spent two years on a substitute teacher list, waiting for an opening to come in the area I wanted to live in, but nothing ever opened up. I actually even once had a placement as an art teacher for an entire year at a middle school, but then at the end of the year, when I applied for the job, I didn't get it. At that point I decided just to fall back on my graphic design degree that I had from college. So, I started to work at a local newspaper. It was horrible. It was expected of us to work overtime that wasn't paid. Then I took another teaching job, where I taught public speaking and how to use Microsoft Office, and then another where I started to teach graphic design, digital pre-press, and 2D and 3D animation.

These were all temporary positions, but then I lucked into a multimedia designer position at a place that built educational software. From that point on, I kind of went from multimedia designer to web designer to User Experience (UX) designer over the course of 10 years and four or five different jobs. I knew immediately when working as a web designer and a User Experience designer that UX was the field that I loved and was passionate about. I naturally gravitated towards work that allowed me to do competitive benchmarking, researching what users did through analytics, and talking to users to figure out how they used our product. That's how I got started in UX.

Looking back, I may have gone overkill with my education. I have three undergraduate degrees, two graduate degrees, and five certifications (now that they exist), and these all are in design, art, User Experience, or interactive design. So, I had a mountain of formal training and I've had years to grow into the field, but UX didn't have a name originally. It wasn't until years later that UX had a profession attached to it, and then college degree programs started offering training in it, and by then I was already working in the field.

Over the years I've worked for nonprofits, for higher education, for e-commerce corporations, for Fortune 500s, and government contractors with varying titles as a User Experience designer, engineer, or architect. I have worked on websites, web applications, Learning Management Systems, enterprise software applications, e-commerce applications, and more. It took me years to learn the many different skills of my field, and I'm still learning every single day. I like to think of myself as a lifelong learner, which marries pretty well to the field of UX, because you're constantly learning as part of the job.

Some of the roadblocks I faced along the way were specifically championing User Experience and user data, and trying to get stakeholders and clients alike to change their minds about how they work. It seems like every place I've worked has always been an uphill battle trying to convince the business or organization of the value of user data, and how it can be worked into their existing processes. It's not until a business or organization starts to see their goals aligning with user goals and starting to get positive feedback, conversion, interaction, or whatever success looks like, that they start to have that 'aha moment' toward the value of User Experience.

The reason I'm writing this book is to make a quick primer that speaks to the things I didn't realize about the UX field, the long-term habits I needed to form and likewise break, and the mistakes I've made that almost killed my career (and could kill someone else's). There are so many articles out on the web about User Experience because the field is growing, and I thought that this was a good way to disseminate knowledge in a fun manner.

When I started to think about these three things – what I didn't realize, what I needed to do, habit wise, to make it in the long term, and what I needed to kill or eliminate for my career – it started to make me think of the very crude game f**k, marry, or kill. So, when I started capturing my thoughts in text and writing this, the book kind of naturally fell into that f**k, marry, or kill cadence.

For me the f**ks really equate to those 'oh f**k' moments I didn't realize initially about the field of User Experience. I wish someone would have told me and that I would have known sooner. The marry part, to me, is really those long-term things that you're going to have to embrace and avoid, and these are daily / weekly things that are going to come up over, and over, and over again. all the time. It's the stuff where you're just going to have to fall on the side of wisdom if you want to have a successful career in this field. And finally, the kill stuff started to really equate to huge mistakes, epic mistakes as a professional that could immediately or over a short amount of time kill and end your career.

So *UX: FMK* just kind of grew out of that mindset. I hope you take this book as a conversation between you and I, as one friend or one colleague to another, and that I can pass on a few things that will be helpful to you as you work in User Experience. Enjoy!

20 F**KS TO GIVE

#1: F**K, WHAT'S THE DIFFERENCE BETWEEN UI AND UX?

I worked with many people over the years that thought User Experience was just a sidecar to web design, and they don't really have a clear understanding of what UX is. In the beginning, I think a lot of people starting out in UX mix it up with User Interface (UI) design. We hear UI and UX used interchangeably, especially in job descriptions, but I think it's important to understand the difference between UI and UX.

It's just one Google search away to find 100 articles, blog posts, or Medium articles stating all the many differences between UI and UX design. I would encourage you first and foremost to familiarize yourself with what UI refers to versus what UX refers to, then you can better speak to the type of skill sets you can bring to a project, and understand other work that needs to be completed as a deliverable. If you don't know, it's 100% certain that you're probably going to run into product people, developers, business analysts, sysadmins, and others who don't know either.

So, you need to educate yourself so you can educate them and clearly describe what the difference is between designing something visually with colors fonts and branding versus UX, which is how the user interacts with and understands the user interface. Even more so when you get to the point of performing UI and UX research, they are two very different things. Likewise, the deliverables for both UI and UX are oftentimes two very different things. Familiarize yourself with the differences so you can understand them and explain them to others.

#2: WHAT THE F**K IS THE UX PROCESS, AND HOW DO I LEARN IT?

A lot of young UXers start out wishing they could better understand the value of instilling and defending a solid process. In general, it's kind of reckless to jump into projects without any type of forethought; without such things as personas, storyboards, user flows, or knowing anything at all about your users or how they're using the product and what they're actually doing.

When I started out my career in User Experience it didn't even have a name, so like a lot of professionals I learned various fields that eventually would be cobbled together into what we now call User Experience. I started out understanding design and desktop publishing and layout color theory... things of that nature which are very visual and I now know are tools in the tool belt that you have to use. I spent some time next as a multimedia designer where I came to understand interaction design, communicating to the user when something's loading or when they need to click. I then learned HTML and CSS and some JavaScript as I started to work on websites. This then propelled me into the digital software life cycle, and with that came an understanding of the agile and lean development processes, what version control tools are, like JIRA, how to communicate with developers as well as different business analysts and products to find out what people need.

It's a lot starting out. It will take some time, so you should know be aware of that, but you should also know that you need to be open and willing to be mentored by others in the field. You need to find skilled people, gravitate towards them, work with them, find out what they're doing, and learn from them. These will be people that, over time, you will keep in touch with and who you'll build lifelong career relationships and, possibly, friendships with, and these are people that will eventually populate your network when you are moving and looking for jobs. So, it's not just a process of studying on your own, it's also learning from the right people.

#3: WHAT THE F**K AM I DOING?!

Anyone who has spent a significant amount of time in UX or who went to school and trained in it will tell you that you need to wear multiple hats. A lot of newbies or green behind the ear kids coming right out of college start working in the industry and think that they will be doing one specific thing, however that's not the case.

Instead of thinking that you're specializing and that you can rely on other professionals to do those types of functions, the truth is that, if anything, you're going to add more and more to the rack (that's a weightlifting term). Meaning, that it's not just going to be research, or design, or css, or translating requirements into user interfaces, it's going to be a lot of different things that you're going to be expected to do. In many instances in UX you're in a position where you are part of a product or service's journey from its beginning stages when it's just an idea or a thought, all l the way through to shipping something out the door, and even after.

Just because the product has launched doesn't mean the process ends. There's always testing, and improving, reiterating, redesigning, expanding to new markets, and adding new features. By being a part of an entire process of a product, or a service, or a software, as a UX professional you need to understand every aspect of that product, software, or service and all of the things it touches. In addition to that you need to be able to communicate ideas across a wide array of disciplines, because you could be working with people who only deal with business requirements, Sprint Cycles, or even finances on the bottom line.

You may not, when you start out, realize the percentage of your day that you will be spending just explaining what you do as a UX designer to other people, and you will have these conversations many times over throughout your career. Unfortunately, that's just the case for UX in the market now. People are starting to understand the value of it, and incorporate it, and grow it, and build even teams for it, or are putting a UX person on a team but you are still going to have to validate your position, you're still going to have to be doing more than what it is you think that your job is about doing, and you're going to have to do many different types of things in the workplace. I think most User Experience professionals after they have some years under their belt would look back and think that maybe they should have taken a public speaking class, maybe they should have taken more statistics or business management courses, because those will pay off for you, and they will definitely be things that you need to do in your day-to-day job.

#4: F**K, I DON'T KNOW WHAT TO DO TO FIND OUT AN ANSWER!

People who are coming to the field of User Experience can come into it from a variety of different backgrounds. Some come from a more artistic or creative director side, where others can come in from development, while still others can come from science or research. Research is something those entering UX would probably do particularly well to understand more formally, or even how to do gorilla research methods.

A lot of times your role as a UX professional is going to be to answer questions when people don't know why something is happening. A UX professional's bread-and-butter is being able to say to someone whose comes to you, "Hey I don't know why this error keeps happening to users when they try to check out," and you being able to reply to that, and say "I don't know either, but I can find out for you."

You will need to understand a lot of different ways to get information; data, analytics, customer feedback, expert perspectives, or any other type of data so that you will be able to flush out and understand problems, then crack solutions to them. Understanding what you can get from analytics is great, but what if you don't have analytics set up and so you have no idea what people are actually doing in the app?

Product people and stakeholders can tell you "We know people are doing this". I always push back and ask "Well how do you know that?" If they have server access logs, or people are calling in and making complaints to a help desk, that's great! That's data that I need, and that is data that you should see to better understand the context of a problem. Being able to get qualitative and quantitative data that's already recorded somewhere is fantastic, but in addition to that you need to know how to create surveys and assessments or conduct research that gets you qualitative and quantitative data when you have none.

The beautiful thing is that we have the internet, which is the sum of all human knowledge, and if you don't know how to get the data you need, you can find out how you can get the data. There's various testing software, there's various analytics platforms, there's various mapping tools – like empathy mapping or Journey mapping – that can help you to understand a process, service, or the user and tell you why something's happening. Use those. You will need them.

#5: F**K, I WANT A UX CAREER PATH!

UX is a pretty amorphous field, and you'll find out that different companies (or even at the same company!) will understand it differently. You can literally have a person at the same company with the same UX title as another person at that company, but they are doing two completely different things. I've heard of UX designers, UX researchers, UX architects, UX developers, and so on and on.

Just like any field, it's important that you have the pay, but also that you're doing what you want. However, you should just abandon any idea of getting the title that you want in UX unless you are fortunate enough to write your own job description and title.

Consistency here just does not exist. Every company does it differently, and even if you have a title that you want — let's say that you are a product User Experience architect and that you worked for years to get that title — no one will refer to you by that. They may call you a product person or a designer, or a UX designer.

So just be okay with the fact that the field is amorphous and ill defined, and don't worry so much about the title. As long as you do the type of work that you like and you're doing solid research and design and including the user into the process at every step, that's great. Just don't sweat the title.

#6: WHAT THE F**K IS THE DATA SHOWING!

One of the tools that I have used forever, and that I never would have thought would be so valuable, is the simple spreadsheet. By-the-book quantitative and qualitative data is something that you're going to be asked to deliver time and time again in your career as a UXer or UX researcher. So, by-the-book quantitative and qualitative analysis techniques are something that you need to become very familiar with.

I tell junior UX professionals this all the time; that getting to know Google Sheets or Microsoft Excel is one of the best things that you can do. When you start to work with data visualization oh, and you will at some point have to work with data visualization, especially if it's your own research, you're going to have to be able to show that data in a tabular format as well as a visualized format. Knowing how to do formulas in Excel, create charts from spreadsheets, and display data findings in a way that's understandable to stakeholders, product development people, or other members of your team is going to be critical.

It's great if you have Google analytics and it makes charts for you. However, most of the time nobody is going to understand those default charts and presets, so you're going to have to cook up some custom charts, custom data visualizations, and custom tabular data displays yourself. You're also going to have to speak in very detailed ways about how you've conducted the research for your qualitative and quantitative data.

You will more than once be questioned whether you have dirty data, that is, if your data collecting techniques were by the book, and your findings will be subject to scrutiny. Double down and find out what good qualitative and quantitative analysis techniques are, and display that data in a way that is irrefutable. This will earn you respect as well as trust in the workplace, which is something you're not going to have by default.

#7: WHAT IS THIS F**KING CODE?!

A big thing that a bunch of junior UX professionals wish that they knew more of going in is the coding side of the user interface. Cap Watkins always says that "designers need to know how to write CSS, and if you disagree then you're wrong, and I'll tell you why... but it'll take an hour." I'm here to tell you that he is 100% correct. You have to know more than just color, fonts, and design.

You need to understand the final form in which your products or services will live, and that can often mean that you need to know HTML, CSS, CSS preprocessor, JavaScript, Polymer, React JS, PHP, Ruby on Rails, or a variety of other coding systems. You are at a disadvantage if you are only working with a design skill set, and people know it. They will know that you're a person that only does marketing mock-ups, that you design emails, you design flyers, and that you design UIs, but don't know anything about interaction or building an actual code.

Don't be this person. Bite the bullet, build yourself your own portfolio website, and this will teach you some beginning skill sets of HTML and CSS. Do not go out and pay for a service like Squarespace or any other website hosting and building place and just use a template. Yes, it saves time, but you don't have a knowledge or skill set that you're building that you can actually show.

By building your own portfolio website, or possibly volunteering for a nonprofit in your area and helping them build a website, you are building a skill set for code. By building a CSS, HTML, and JavaScript skillset, those three coding languages can cross apply to a bunch of different things that you're going to interact with over the years, and will help you understand how to speak like a developer speaks.

#8: LISTEN TO ME F**KERS!

For a new person coming into the field of UX, one of the tips I can give you is to shut up, and become a better listener.

I'll tell you this now and you may not believe it, but listening and communicating is 75% of the work you're going to do as a UXer. Being able to listen, understand the problem, and understand what deliverables are needed under what time lines and parameters is essential for you as a UX professional. A lot of newbie or junior UX professionals wish they had better skills at taking notes, listening, presenting, and being an influencer.

By listening, taking notes, and talking and asking questions, you are building your understanding of everyone's needs, what the parameters are, and what the deliverables are. That's where people need you. They need you in a place or location where you're informed, you understand what every team's doing, and you can figure out how you can best plug-in to that process or provide what is needed.

What people don't need is an artsy-fartsy designer, who nobody really understands, going off and creating something beautiful on their own, especially when it's not what the team needed or asked for. This is why UX professionals have an uphill battle and a bad name, because they're considered to be those artsy creative people who go off and do something, and then they bring back what they want someone else to build.

Every developer snickers and complains about that person. Don't be that person. Listen to what people say, ask for clarification when you don't understand, research, look at documentation, and look at requirements. You will then be in a position where you better understand the service or product, and how to better be effective as a UX professional to achieve business goals.

#9: MEET ME IN THE PARKING LOT, F**KER!

The aphorism "choose your battles wisely" exists for a reason.

Over the years I've written several articles and spoken on various podcasts about choosing your battles wisely as a UX professional. This is a skill that you need to develop quickly and you need to realize that UX is not the center of the universe. By choosing your battles wisely you don't waste energy on everything, because you can't win every single battle. It's just not possible.

The truth is as, as a UXer you're going to come in contact with very difficult people in the workplace. You might have hellish clients, project managers, or even stakeholders that micromanage, bottleneck communications, or simply presume they already understand everything. In those cases where you do need to do battle, and as a rule of thumb it should be about 30% of the time versus 70% of the time not caring, letting it go, and letting someone else make the decision.

When you do pick a UX battle you need to safely be able to negotiate that terrain. Just like the old man from the 1986 video game *The Legend of Zelda* who warns you "it's dangerous to go alone," throughout your career you will meet people (swords) that you need to take with you to battle on these teams. This can be a fellow team member, it could just be another person working on the project, it could even be a supervisor. If you're the only UXer on a team who has to defend your decisions to an entire team you need to get allies on your side. Simply having another perspective, or set of eyes and ears can reduce miscommunication, increase your defense, and eliminates being sidelined or surprise attacked. You'll be surprised how much more smoothly meetings go then if you have a person with you.

For the other 30% of the time you need allies and you need to make a choice if it's worth fighting or not. These choices will be informed by determining and then applying an appropriate level of effort. Sometimes the level of effort may be small, sometimes the level of effort is large, but you will need to ask yourself if styling a button or using a specific font is worth the overly difficult arguments or confrontations. Sometimes you need to run away so you can fight another day.

#10: WHO F**KED THIS UP?!

Sometimes you're going to be pulled onto projects, especially as a junior UX professional, and you're going to quickly realize that nobody knows what they're doing. Maybe there have been no solidified requirements, maybe the team doesn't understand what the business goal or intent is. Sometimes user stories have never been written, or not derived from research, or, even worse, no one did any research by talking to a user.

In these situations, you need to have an outline to which you can refer. This outline is going to cover a base level of where you need to come in and what you need to do. Every UXer makes an outline over time and it's kind of their bread and butter that they refer to, and this is sometimes referred to as your UX 'bags of tricks'.

You will need to come up with your outline yourself but as a starting point number one is always:

1. **Getting on the same page.** This means that everyone needs to understand the OKRs (objectives and key results), the KPIs (key performance indicators), and the customer life-cycle. This is simply where you have to start, and if you don't know these, then you need to define them. There are many exercises available to teach you how to do this, and a great one is in Laura Klein's book *Build Better Products: A Modern Approach to Building Successful User-Centered Products*. This will get you all on the same page, realize what your goals are, realize what success looks like, and how you'll actually sell and

market a product or service.

2. **What do we know and how do we know it?** This is about asking yourself "what quantitative and qualitative data do we have already, and if we don't have any then how do we get some?"

3. **How do we know how to improve the service or product?** How do we acquire pain points from users, how do we conduct system usability scales? Maybe we need to conduct a usability audit that identifies problems with screenshots, or maybe we need to conduct peer evaluation or competitive benchmarking. If you don't know who your peers are, and you don't even have a baseline of how your product compares against other products, then that's a problem.

4. **Defining parameters for improving the product.** This can be brainstorming, ideating, discussing possibilities, discussing a minimum viable product, or minimum viable experience. There are ways to get the team together to generate ideas of what they would like to see, what they would like to do, and then you can kind of weigh those against business needs and goals to see which ones match up. As a UXer what you want here is to align user goals to business goals. That's a win-win situation.

#11: WHY IS THERE A F**KING DISCONNECT?

When you start out as a junior UXer, you're going to find out that you wish you had been better prepared for the disconnect between how your field views User Experience and how the world views User Experience. Now don't get me wrong, UXers have done a great job defining this field and connecting the disconnected, but people still misconstrue and misinterpret User Experience.

Just like how people confuse UI and UX you're going to encounter a lot of very opinionated people that have strong feelings and perspectives about what it is you should be doing. The best advice I can give you is to take this as an opportunity to help educate those people and let them know what skill sets you have, and what competencies you can bring to each team.

By approaching the situation this way, you're going to help people understand User Experience, but also create the perception of value in what you do. Unfortunately, this is going to be a disconnect you're going to face a lot, and I'm sure it's not going to change anytime soon.

Because of the crazy job titles, people are not going to know from your job title what it is you do. You're going to have to tell them, and you're going to have to go a step beyond that by explaining how it is that you can help the team when they think that you and your skill sets are not beneficial.

#12: WHY IS IT F**KING IMPORTANT TO KNOW WHAT SUCCESS LOOKS LIKE?

It's great to have the user in mind, and it's great to tout all of the things that you can do with user research because you observed or talked or tested some users. However. you're never, ever going to be in a situation where it doesn't matter if you're selling a product, or if conversion is happening.

You need to understand business goals, what success looks like, and how the business makes money. If you don't know how the business makes money, then how do you know how you plug into the greater scheme, what your goal is, and what you need to do on a daily basis to help the business succeed? In the end you're being paid for a job, and UX is just a job like any other. If you cannot do your job because you don't care enough about how the business makes money, people are going to know that. You need to marry user goals to business goals, which will not always happen, but when it does happen, it's a win-win.

Most of the time people shoot from the hip, they do their own thing, they just kind of figure out where they think they should go, and what direction they should navigate… but what you can bring to the table is research and data from users to help guide that. Why would any business want to pay you every two weeks with a paycheck if you're not really involved with how the business makes money, and you don't want the business to succeed?

What you need to do is stop thinking of UX as this creative thing that you do off by yourself and that no one else can do it, because you'll get skipped over, not invited to meetings, and no one will listen to you. What you need to do is talk to people, understand the business, and ask people at every level, "What does success look like?" What success looks like for a developer, versus what success looks like for a business owner are two very different things. You need to know both so you can navigate both worlds and provide the best support to your products and services as a UX professional.

#13: AM I F**KING UP THE RESEARCH?

Most likely, starting out in UX you're not going to know what good research and strategy practices are. Before UX became a discipline, people came from web design, statistics, or research. A lot of people came from graphic design positions where they were wrangling pixels all day. One of the most important things that you need to understand when conducting usability testing, which is evaluating a product or service by testing it with users, is not to bias your research or lead the users to what you want them to do.

You should write usability testing scripts. You should write them and write them often. Then you should evaluate those testing scripts at a later time. You know, come back to it, let it sit after writing it, and then a day later come back (or hours later) and just look at it and see if you're leading the user to the answer. An example of this is: instead of phrasing something in such a way as, "show me how you would search for a toy using this website," ask yourself if you're saying something like "go to the search bar typing 'toys' and then press enter." That's bad! What you have just done is given the user a solution on how to do something.

The insights that come out of usability testing are never expected. Even after the many times that I've conducted usability testing, I always find something unexpected, where I notice something that I just never thought I would encounter. These are the golden moments that you're looking for. You could set out trying to find why users are encountering a particular error, and you want to see if it's user errors or instruction errors, but you could encounter a bug where a modal is covering up a section of the webapp, and you never would have known that if you led the user to click on a certain box and type in a certain thing.

So, don't f**k up your research! Write your testing scripts in a very neutral way that do not lead the user to a specific answer. In the end you will get better insights, you will get more useful results, and you will not be accused of muddying up the waters or misleading a user during a usability test.

#14: Do they expect me to know f**king everything?

The answer is, emphatically, no. Junior UX professionals should know that you will not be expected to know everything about your field. It's 100% okay to say, "I don't know, but I can find out" or "let me look into that for you." Yes the perception from your team could be that you're expected to be an expert in the UX skill set, and that you should in turn give the best direction and guidance based off of your research, your knowledge, and your skill-set; however, it's probably going to be very helpful for you to know right now that it's okay not to know information. It's okay to say that you have not figured it out, and be able to speak with confidence and transparency as to what it is you're doing.

One of the aphorisms that I hate and loathe is "fake it till you make it." I hate the saying because it sounds like you're lying all the time, when in fact you could be learning as you go instead. So what I would say is when you don't understand something, ask questions and if you're not sure exactly how to go about fixing a problem, re-searching a solution or conducting a usability test it's okay.

You can search the Fountain of Knowledge that is the internet, and you'll find information there that will specifically tell you "Hey, this is where you need to do a service or empathy map," or "You should conduct user Diaries, or a focus group." You can also look at articles written by other UXers that are going to tell you where you need a style guide, or where a pattern library would help. Once you en-counter these things, that's a tool that you've just added to your tool belt, and as you go through your career your toolbelt becomes larger, has more tools in it, and you become more proficient at using the tools. You may not be there yet, but you can get there, and that's okay to say and communicate.

#15: WHAT THE F**K IS A LOE?

Starting out you may not be tasked with multiple projects, however soon enough in your career you're going to have to start juggling. You could be juggling a project that needs a style guide on the left, but then on the right you need to conduct user research, but then something else pops up that requires you to translate user interfaces into high fidelity or interactive mock-ups. You may be pulled in to translate requirements into user interfaces and collaborate with development.

In all these instances, what you need to be able to do is apply the appropriate level of effort and know the correct tool to use. We talked a little bit before about level of effort (LOE), but what you need to understand is some tools are overkill, and you do not need to dive into a brand new tool you know nothing about or a brand new software application when you have something due in two days. You will not have the time to learn a new software as well as complete what you need to do.

So what you need to do is think of the level of effort you can apply in regards to the time, and then choose a software or tool appropriately. It's 100% okay to whiteboard some drawings and concepts, and photograph those to present in a team meeting. It's okay to use sticky notes to capture questions that you may have instead spending time seeking what the answers are. If you have time to do low-fidelity wireframes in Balsamiq, Axure, or another software like Google Draw, that's okay too. What people are going to respond to in the team that you're working with is the knowledge that you're making progress in your moving forward. They don't really care so much about the fidelity of your prototypes or how you're capturing questions. If your team can understand drawings, then draw if that's what you can do. Later, if you have time to translate your drawings into wireframes do it, but you need to focus on the 'meat and potatoes' of a problem before focusing on the garnish.

Now there will also be projects that you encounter where you have more time and can maybe spend months or years on them, and in those instances that's where you should loop in a new software. That's where you should learn Adobe XD, Axure, Balsamiq, or a new tool that you've wanted to try out. That's 100% okay... but you don't want to do that when you're on a very specific timeline.

So, don't sabotage yourself by throwing yourself into a new software. Use the tools that you know to get the job done, and then, if the request is for something high fidelity, then just communicate "I'm not familiar with that tool, but if we can do something at lower fidelity, like drawings or low fidelity wireframes, then if you give me more time I can translate it to high-fidelity." It's okay to communicate you don't know how to use a tool, but it's 100% not okay to not do work and let your team see that you're just screwing around with fonts or colors because you don't understand the software application.

#16: WHEN THE F**K WILL YOU BE DONE?

Multiple times throughout your career as a UX professional you're going to be asked to estimate UX or give estimates when a deliverable will be ready. When starting out as a UXer you probably will not know what those time frames are, and that's okay. Different products and demands will involve varying levels of complexity and will require you to use different technologies or methods. Also, some projects will require you to use tools that you may not currently know how to use.

An example of this is designing a good commercial web page for a Fortune 500 company versus designing the user interface for medical equipment. When you look online it can seem like many blog articles and videos say you should do everything the same way. However, in reality that may not be the case at all. You will need to take time to find out how long it will take you to deliver the goods.

If someone asks you in a meeting, or peer pressures you to say how long something will take – and this happens a lot in agile software scrum meetings or sprint planning – here's the one thing you need to know: if someone says to you, "I need to know the hours to put on this ticket that I'm assigning you to do wireframes... how many hours is it going to take?" It's okay to say, "I can't tell you because I don't know, and I haven't dived into it yet, so I cannot speak to something I don't know... so if you want to assign an arbitrary number that's on you, but I can't speak to that."

I'm more comfortable saying, "Hey this is a sprint, give me the sprint to do it that's two weeks... 80 hours and we'll put that on it... but I can't tell you anything more than that at this time." It's okay to communicate to people that you can't give an exact time, but you can give an estimate.

The problem here is that at the beginning of your career as a UXer you're not going to know how much time it's going to take you to do most things. So always overestimate is my advice to you. Overestimate every single time you can overestimate for all the time you can. This gets you two things:

1. One it **gives you more time** so if something is more complex and you need more time to do it you've just given yourself time.

2. The second thing it gives you is this: **if you get things done quicker it creates the perception that, "oh I can do stuff faster and deliver it ahead of schedule."** That's a great reputation to have and that's a great perspective for your co-workers to have of you. So, overestimate and deliver early; that's the best thing that you can do.

#17: HOW BIG IS THIS F**KING TEAM?

There are many different types of work situations in UX, ranging from small mom-and-pop businesses, to big corporations, to nonprofits, to contracting, to subcontracting work. It's all going to be different and every UX structure at every place is going to be different. I wish I could tell you that it's going to be the same and consistent, but that's simply not the case.

You may join a team that has no other UX professionals or designers or researchers and you may be filling all three rolls. Typically, this is a nightmare, because you'll be expected to do the job of four people. In other instances, you may be one of many UXers assigned to a specific product or widget, and even then, you won't have real contact with other UX professionals even though you work with 20 in the same building. Another possibility is that you could work on a UX team, and on this team, you have various number of members and work comes into you through a queue or it's entirely possible that each member of the team has a domain in addition to work coming in.

In all of these different instances, however, what's important is how you are receiving the work, how people contact you, and how you're spending your time. One of the principles of lean UX or just lean software development in general is that you minimize the multiple ways that everyone can request work from you. If you are getting work – no matter if you're on a team or an individual – if you're receiving requests from email, from a ticketing system, from instant messaging, from a work request form, etc. that's way too many ways you're receiving work. You may not be able to change that, but hopefully you can try to have all the work go through one funnel.

If you can use a Kanban board just to manage your own work it is going to be a benefit for you. This way you can actually see what work is on your plate, what work is due when, and what the status of certain projects is.

Another thing; you'll want to block out your calendar. The larger the company you work for the more bullsh*t meetings you're going to be expected to attend. Essentially, I've worked at a place before where people would schedule meetings before 8 a.m. all the way till 5:00 p.m. and then over lunch. It was ridiculous, and it went on for years until finally enough people b*tched about it and the technology office put blockers on people's calendars for the whole corporation so no one could schedule meetings over lunch, before 8 a.m., or after 4 p.m.

Do not rely on such blockers. When you know you need to do schedule blocks of time in your calendar where you are unavailable so you can complete your work. Do this as much as you need. This is the only way to ensure that people are not scheduling meetings with you and you can get your work completed.

#18: BUT, I'M A GREAT F**KING DESIGNER!?

One thing people who start out in UX wish they would have known is that being a great designer, or even the best designer, doesn't mean you can always tackle a problem and come up with a solution.

You will need to be able to facilitate conversations about the research, data, and requirements. Facilitating design thinking is one of the skill sets that you want to have as a feather in your cap. You need to be able to pull out a great solution from a group of people, and you do this by facilitating conversations to understand the problem, to understand potential forms of architecture, or how users do something, and capturing all of those in notes and verbal communication.

I take notes vigorously on every single meeting, and I record them and concatenate them. This is something you should do. You can refer back to those notes, synthesize insights from them, capture data from what people said in meetings, and those can feed into the solutions that you propose.

Being able to go to a stakeholder who simply wants a thing done in a certain way, and being able to facilitate how they would do this by having them draw on the board and show you how they would do this or how they would visualize this is a necessary skill.

I was specifically asked by a business stakeholder to do a chart in a certain way that didn't make sense, so when I met with them I asked, "Can you please take this marker and draw on this whiteboard and show me what it is that you're talking about?" The business owner scoffed at the idea and thought they were above it, but I pleaded again, "Please humor me" and I facilitated him doing this with different colors and markers on the whiteboard. He soon found out the problem that I was encountering by drawing out the chart that he wanted to see. By him actually going through the process, and by facilitating going through the process he understood what he was asking for was impossible.

Being able to facilitate capturing problems, understanding processes, or facilitating focus groups or team conversations is also going to be a part of your bread and butter. When you are working specifically with service mapping, you will be alarmed how one, two, or three people think that they know what's going on, but when you get them in the same room talking to one another they do not realize that there is a crucial step in the process where one of them needs to do something . That's why people do service mapping, service blueprinting, or journey mapping, because you need to facilitate a group's understanding of how an entire system works. Otherwise people won't know, and it will just be overlooked, and when something's redesigned you're going to encounter those problems anyway. So just facilitate those conversations now and you'll be able to better capture data and come up with solutions.

#19: AM I GOING TO F**KING DO THIS FOREVER?

A lot of UXers probably do not realize the smaller the company they work for, the more mundane the UX work is going to be. I typically find out within two to four years, and sometimes it's even less, maybe one year or 6 months, what it is I'm going to be doing, day in and day out for the rest of my life. That's a hard, sobering fact for people to face.

In UX it can be very monotonous if you become the wireframe person, and all you do all day long, every day, every week, all year make wire frames. You will go crazy. You will go f**king insane, and you will take your whole team with you.

Just realize that your current company or business's understanding of UX is going to grow, but essentially the job skills or job requirements may not. If you work for an advertising newspaper, you're going to be doing pagination all day, every single day, putting together ads for ad reps. That's what you're going to be doing today, tomorrow, and 5 years from now.

So maybe understand what it is you want to do and where you want to be in the future, and then try to stomach your work until you can actually start doing or getting a job that allows you to do the UX work that you want to do.

The one thing that is exciting and enticing about working at a larger Corporation or company with UX is that there's going to be a whole Myriad of tasks. Some companies will need style guides, some projects at the company will need testing, where others maybe need wireframes, others need requirements or research, and it's great being able to juggle a lot of different balls... if that's what you want to do. I know very few UX people who actually want to design all day long. I think that would get boring, and you may too.

However, if you know that for the next 40 years you want to design mock-ups and you love it, then by all means f**king do it, but I just don't think that is sustainable for any person. So, either look for opportunities at your current work to expand and communicate to your supervisors and bosses how you want to grow. If a year or two has gone by and you haven't had a conversation with your boss or immediate supervisor about how your career is going and how you want it to grow with regard to the company, then you need to leave that f**king company, because it's never going to change and the type of work you want is never going to come. In the end you'll thank yourself.

#20: Do the F**king Work!

There's another old aphorism that goes, 'doing the work makes you good at the work'... or something like that. The truth is, the only way to get good at UX, and the different skill-sets required by UX, is by actually doing it.

I know the internet is completely full of list based articles, or listicles as they're often called, but I would actually say that you have six UX skill categories or skill sets that you need to build confidence in, and the only way to do that is by actually doing the f**king work in thos six categories. You will see, just like a lot of UX professionals, that your field is misunderstood. You will be annoyed by it, and you will try to blame others. However, the blame is kind of shared between all of us, because UX professionals have allowed and championed certain perspectives of the field, and we have riddled the internet with articles about what skills make up UX.

My understanding of UX is constantly evolving and ever-changing. I'm a lifelong learner, and if you are a UX professional and you truly love the field, you're going to be a lifelong learner too. I've been working in the field of UX for almost 20 years and specifically doing UX for software development for half that time. From my vantage point, everything that a UXer or UX team can or will be asked to do can be placed into six skill categories. These are the six areas that you will need to do work in to actually learn, and understand, and grow by doing the work:

- Business Skills
- Content Strategy Skills

- Design Thinking Skills
- Development Skills
- Research Skills
- Visual Design Skills

For business skills you will need to understand key performance indicators (KPIs), what success looks like for the business, and the needs of the stakeholders. For content strategy; doing content audits, card sorts increasing findability and discoverability, redoing navigation and information architecture will build that skill. Design thinking skills will encompass you facilitating design thinking and understanding, mapping requirements, concept mapping with a group of people, or service blueprinting. Development skills is essentially programming; CSS, HTML, and JavaScript and how to use them through version control and repositories and get systems. Research skills are going to be something you have to grow by actually conducting usability tests, screening for remote users, writing test scripts, and so on. And your visual design skills are something you're going to have to grow by actually doing graphic design, visual communication, or understanding the elements and principles of design (fyi there are seven each).

By doing this work you grow your skill sets. By doing just particularly designed work, you're letting the other five skill sets not develop. You need to diversify yourself.

20 Lessons in Marriage

#1: Marry into other families!

A long-term habit that you will want to form that'll give you a healthy career as a UX professional is that it's good to look outside of your field.

Yes, you can look at other design disciplines for inspiration, but look even further outside of that. One of the things that I get very excited about when I see them done well are infographics. For me, that's something that I derive a lot of inspiration from, because well done infographics are easily digestible, understandable, and help explain something foreign to a user. Another reason I like infographics is because they do a lot to visualize big data, and they don't mock the viewer for their lack of understanding about the subject. More so, they educate the user in easily understandable ways through how information is displayed. Infographics don't have to be your thing, it's just my thing.

You need to get inspiration outside of your field. That could be from infographics, it could be from video games, or it could be from something else. Video games are often another source I refer to for great micro interactions, information architecture, and interaction models. There are times that very large enterprise web applications could be much better designed if they would only embrace the user interface of a video game controller in their menu system.

You need to look outside of your field for experience, draw creativity from that field, and it will invigorate your work. Have you looked at board games, theatre, television, roleplaying games, podcasts, or movies?

#2: IF YOU LIKE THAT WIREFRAME SO MUCH, WHY DON'T YOU MARRY IT!

Even though wireframes are a great way to decompose requirements and translate them to user interface, it's possible to spend too much time creating and drawing wireframes.

Don't get me wrong wireframes are definitely the entry point for user interface, and everyone wants razzle-dazzle. They want to see color, they want to see fun, they want to see the bright and shiny things that they can click on (e.g. animation and interaction). However, as a UX person don't get in the habit of doing nothing but wireframes all the time.

There are so many other things that you can do as a UX professional concerning data, research, data visualization, and documentation just to name a few. For example, a valuable tool in your belt is going to be instructional design strategy. Instructional design strategy is going to be integrated with a wireframe, and that's something that you need to learn, and familiarize yourself with; especially how it operates in other applications or in services.

You will need to integrate tooltips, ask yourself how can text help in app manuals, or even wizards that walk users through a step-by-step process. Building a wire frame for a wizard or contextual help is great, but what a team is really going to need, especially if they only have you, the UX person, and they don't have the instructional designer or content strategist, they're going to need you to step up and fill the role as an instructional designer, technical writer, or UX writer. Don't be afraid to do this. This is something that you will never be asked to do, but everyone will appreciate it when you do it.

Likewise, accessibility is something that no one likes to own, and they rarely have an accessibility expert on a team, so as a UX professional you need to step up and encompass accessibility in your work. If you don't speak to instructional design or accessibility concerns in your wireframes, because everyone's going to see the wire frames, then no one is ever going to be concerned about how users learn or how users with disabilities operate the application you're designing.

#3: ARE WE MARRIED TO NOT CONDUCTING RESEARCH?

It is often said that our product is 'only as good as the data we have'. You're going to find out that a lot of the time companies want to bypass the research stage of a project. Mike Monteiro, the co-founder and design director of *Mule Design*, in his book *Design is a Job,* specifically has an entire chapter devoted to making time for research.

Monteiro posits that when you get a new client and you have to research, the client often times is going to tell you that hey we've already done this research for you, we're just going to hand you the documents, so we don't need to worry about it, and it doesn't affect our timeline.

I will say what Mike says, and that is that it's bullsh*t. Companies, often times, truly believe that they know better than the user, and it takes you and your team time to go through research, see where it has holes, and then add to that research, or point out where the holes are that you need to fill. In a lot of UX professions you're going to find you can waste time and make a lot of mistakes, but having a lack of information, a lack of access for users, and a lack of research that you need to conduct will prohibit you from making a useful product.

The goal in the attention economy, which is what we currently are in, is to make products that users actually want to use or need to use. We want to do this in the simplest way possible, and without having hectic or crazy user interfaces. By conducting your own research, and not allowing your stakeholders or your clients to muscle you into skipping that step, you will be in a better position to build a better product, simple as that.

When you short change the research step, what you're going to find out is that there may have been something that you completely missed. Possibly how the app you're creating for hospital nurses will never see use because a piece of research you didn't conduct or didn't have the time to conduct was a key indicator of what you needed to produce. Don't make that error, and don't fall into the habit of not conducting research or making time for research.

#4: MARRY INTO POWER!

If you ask any seasoned UXer, they're going to tell you that influencing not just design, but also UX within a large organization is a very steep mountain to climb for a lot of UX professionals.

Design doesn't always have a seat at the table, and it isn't until recently that we've started to see chief design officers who have a CO level equivalent to a chief information officer (CIO), chief executive officer (CEO), or similar position. If you actually have the benefit of working at a company that has a chief design officer, or even better a CXO, which is a chief experience officer like a lot of hospitals have – but in hospitals are actually more focused on patient experience and not any of their software or services – count yourself lucky because you're at a company that's ahead of the curve.

However, for everyone else, you are going to have to find and consider a more strategic way to drive influence for UX and design, and you're going to have to find a way to communicate that and make it visible to leaders. Leaders are not always going to know what you do, and if you are just a pixel pusher in their eyes, even when you're actually helping increase conversion by changing User Experience for the way customers check out in an e-commerce website, you need to take the time step back and communicate the good that you do.

This is not just you flouting your accomplishments, but more so it's driving influence and making it visible to others. You need to communicate to leaders that you have a right to be at the table because your decisions are important, and you need to create the constant understanding on their part that you're a valuable asset.

#5: Marry Me, Screamed The User!

A long-term habit that you want to start forming as a UXer is being able to interact with users and get user data to develop insights that improve services and products. However, it is possible to waste a lot of time focusing on the specifics that users say, or just on the users in general, and not enough on the business's needs.

Furthermore, it can be said that you can waste a lot of time focusing specifically on the user, maybe through focus groups or user shadowing, to find out what their daily gripes are and their proclivities. But don't forget that you're there on the part of a business to get insights and user data that translate back to mapping to the business's goals.

Throughout my career, I've heard developers say many times, "Are we just going to do everything that users say because, that seems like a super bad idea," and they would be right. If you build everything that the users said and you polled 50 users for ideas, I would say 3/4 of the ideas are probably bad. The one quote that I like and use a lot of the time is from Steve Jobs wherein he says, "A lot of the time, people don't know what they want until you show it to them." Where this is kind of true and applies to you as a UX professional, is that you have to kind of wade through the bullsh*t that is your users; what their pain points are at their job, and what they dislike, which they'll be fixated on because they'll b*tching about it to you openly.

You have to remember just like Floyd from the Muppets band says, "Just play the gig, man… never get involved in politics." You're there to get insights and data to help improve a product that they don't even know exists. Some of the best-intentioned products and services completely fail because they do exactly what users say to do, thinking that, "Hey, we did exactly what they said, and so this is got to be perfect right?" And then they end up building a product that is unusable and that nobody wants.

This is because product members and User Experience professionals specifically got their marching orders from a user, and instead of extrapolating from a user, a user interview, or focus groups what it is we actually needed to build. So, a good habit is to get all of that information from a user, but then temper it with business understanding, objectives, and deadlines to get what you really need. You may have a bunch of great ideas that users come up with but you may not be able to build them in the timeline that you have, or especially for a minimum viable product (MVP) that's due in six weeks.

#6: LOOK AT ME, I MARRIED HELVETICA TO MATERIAL DESIGN!

A bad habit you would like avoid forming as a UX professional is losing buckets, and buckets of time showing others how many tools you know and how you can make a wireframe look outstanding instead of focusing on actual usability.

I'm a visual person, and I'm assuming you are a visual person too. I like the visual field, I like art, and I like design, and I like gaming, and all of these are things that I'm very geeky about. I also know that I can spend a large amount of time touring fonts and choosing through the best font out of 100 fonts that I find online or creating color palettes for a style guide. I can spend hours and hours doing this because I like typography, and I like color theory, and I like design. However, this is not a habit that a UX person should be putting a lot of time into. If you want to be pegged as a designer, and a designer who only makes pretty pictures then that's the Avenue you want to go down.

For everyone else who's considered being a competent and experienced UX professional this is something you will not want to waste a lot of time on. If you do like this, that's okay. Maybe you should just be a user interface designer or a graphic designer. That's 100% okay but that is not what a UX professional or a UX designer does.

One of the best quotes from Hoa Loranger of the *Nielsen Norman Group* concerning UX is "User Experience without users isn't UX… it's X, which means don't do it." What this quote means is: without being involved with users, or conducting usability testing with users, or user testing, you are not a UXer. If you are just working with co-lors, fonts, and design all day and you're not talking to users, resear-ching, and using user data, then you're just designing in a bubble and shooting from the hip, you're not doing UX design.

So, the habit you want to form is to not spend too much time on the design. A couple years ago I went to *UXcamp* in Washington DC, and one of the presenters there demoed a project that the developers at Pinterest were working on, and it would allow someone who draws a simple set of UI drawings on a whiteboard, to transform that auto-matically into code.

In that moment I knew that the future of UX is not going to be in design, pushing pixels, choosing colors, and fonts... even though that does have some place. Because what we need is functional first, and UX is about what works for the users, not just what looks pretty.

#7: DID YOU MARRY THE WRONG TEST?

A good habit that you want to form over the course of your career is knowing and applying the appropriate research method to a particular query. Not knowing the appropriate research method to apply and to make informed design decisions will cripple you.

This is something that comes with time, it comes with experimenting, and it comes with experience. Knowing when to make a service blueprint to track how the physical world, a digital project, and a user all work together is something you may not know coming right out of college as a junior UX professional. Likewise, you may not know how to get from making an empathy map to creating epics and user stories in JIRA tickets, but it's completely possible, and it's done all the time by UX professionals.

Knowing the difference between qualitative and quantitative research methods is also something you may not know right out of the gate, or that when you're conducting a usability test which is more qualitative you typically only need 5 users to test, whereas when you're wanting something that's more quantitative and you're trying to confirm something numerically you want about 250 people to do a survey result.

You'll have to spend time and make it a habit of learning and understanding what types of research methods to use to get what types of data to answer problems, and not just any problems, but complex problems that people are looking to you, as a User Experience professional to answer. What you can get from Google Analytics as well as Adobe Test and Target, and what is actually being mapped or clicked is something that you should have input on. You may need to work with developers to tag errors, or buttons or links to see when users actually click on them in a user interface or web application. This way you will know where users are going and what they're doing.

I would highly recommend you read *Rubik: Creating a UX resource for the design community* by Cheryl Paulsen. It's an article wherein she kind of unpacks and describes a survey that she built that anyone can use right now. She really does a great job of unpacking what it is that you want to do through user research, whether through questions and answers or through multiple choice. She asks you what you like to learn in your research, and you can choose. Maybe I want to explore user motivations, or I want to explore solutions, or I want to validate something. Essentially it allows a UXer to find out what types of design or user research to conduct. You should go read it now, it will start to make sense, and over time you will learn and know what types of research to conduct to get the data you need.

#8: WHY DID I MARRY INTO THIS IT TEAM?

A lot of the time, you're going to find that, in large companies, as a UXer working on large development teams, you will by default be thrown into an information technology (IT) team or a dev team. However, and this changes case-by-case and Company by company, saddling up with marketing, operations, or sales teams may be more advantageous to you.

This is not to say that you cannot find a great home with an IT or development team, but more so I'm speaking to the fact that such teams too often receive requirements and tickets and log work accordingly. As a product person described to me many years ago, a lot of developers work specifically as mechanics, meaning that they're assigned one specific job, they do that job, and then they move on to the next thing. This is not to say that they don't understand UX, or that they don't want their product to be used by users and for it to have the best usability; but how they generally operate is on the mechanic level of repair and implementation.

However, with marketing, sales, or, what's most likely, products teams, you'll tend to have a customer focus, which means you also tend to have a user focus. The people who are going to be talking to clients that are customers or potential users are going to be your product people. Maybe your marketing people or your salespeople can get you access to users to test and they could answer those questions.

The dev team is oftentimes on their own, and they are micromanaged in regards to their time and their work through sprint planning, stand-ups, technical exchanges, estimating the hours for tickets, and logging time to tickets. It's almost as if they are in a dark pit and, when they're up against a deadline, people will just keep throwing pizza and Mountain Dew into the pit, or potentially throw more developers into the pit to get the job done... but it's kind of hard to talk to users and conduct user research when you're in a pit with the dev team.

I do want to say that you will run into some fantastic developers that you work with, and, depending on your company's makeup and if it's matrix or not, you may have great developers who also want to be involved with the users. I've worked in these situations but the majority of the time in an agile software development cycle, since agile is kind of dead, this will never be the concern of a development team. So, the long-term goal for you here is to find out which team is going to get you the users that you need. If it's development go with dev, but, often times, it's going to be product, marketing, or sales.

#9: MARRY OR DIVORCE PAIN POINTS!?

I will also caution you that as a junior UX professional you do not want to get into the habit of solving problems that don't exist for users. You may get pulled in on various redesign projects, and when you look at it you could think to yourself, "My God this is a legacy web app! It's horrible! It needs to be redesigned, it looks ugly, all the type is small, all the forms look like they're from the 1990s…" Etc.

However, you should ask yourself if you're missing key information from weak discovery phases. Meaning, that you just jumped to solutions based on what you're visually seeing, but you didn't actually conduct any type of design research, competitive benchmarking, understanding of the business goals, or any user research for pain points.

Do you know what value you're bringing? Do you even know what problems you are fixing for the user? You need to do concept deconstructions before proceeding with prototyping. It's okay to have a mood board to get ideas and to put those ideas together and share them, that's what a moodboard is for, however jumping to a solution based on nothing more than your own design preferences is really glossing over what pain points the existing users might have.

You need to get into the trenches, talk to existing users and sales reps, and even people who work the help desk and find out what the problems are, which problems happen the most, and what are the biggest pain points for all the users of the system… not just one type of user.

A system could have users, admins, super admins, operators, analysts, etc. You need to find out what all of their pain points are to propose a solution. Designing from the hip based on your own personal preference is like shooting at fish in a barrel with the lights off. Turn the d*mn light on, take the lid off the barrel, and then shoot!

#10: YOU CAN'T MARRY US, YOU'RE NOT A UXER!

Another habit you want to form is staying away from arguing over who is or who isn't a UXer. In addition to this, arguing over the right way to do things is also a waste of time. You can spend your time arguing and whining as to why UX is great or it sucks, you can argue over if UX professionals should code or not, and so on, and on. Do not spend too much time drawing lines in the sand and playing gatekeeper. No one likes it when you encounter this anywhere else, so why do you think people would like it when they encounter it with you, the sole UX professional or UX team?

Your focus should be on finding a process that works, that alleviates your user's problems, and increases usability. What you just did for your last project as a UX professional may not work for this project. Some of the worst memories I have as a UX professional are sitting in meetings and watching people debate over who owns the UX of a sales website. Product said that they own it, merchandising replied and said, no, they own it, and then the head of eCommerce came in and said both were wrong and they owned it. Meanwhile the entire UX team was in that meeting and was never even spoken to. Finally the supervisor of the UX team stood up and said, "I'm the supervisor of the UX team, and I'm pretty concerned about how everyone thinks that they own UX but no one actually does UX practice." The room went silent, because she was right and everyone was floored.

It's childish to witness other teams falling apart arguing and reverting to such territorialism. The focus should be that all the teams are working together and that they have the best interests of the service or product in mind, not whether they own something, or whether you can touch that door since you don't have such and such approval. This is especially insulting when none of the other teams even had a UX professional working on their team.

Don't fall into this type of arguing, and, when you see it, nip it in the bud. I personally have been in a situation where a product owner told me "That's my decision, I control the User Experience of the app." To which I replied "Well then why aren't you doing the wire frames, conducting the research, or doing the data synthesis?"

So, instead of focusing on territorialism, why don't we talk about what's in the best interest of the project and put this conversation in a sidebar? It doesn't need to exist in the first place, because if you're just wanting to flex your muscles and show that you are in command, that's not the type of team I want to work on. And neither should you.

#11: MARRY YOUR CRAFT IN FRONT OF PERSONAS!

It's possible for UX people to misunderstand what UX is specifically and just associate it with user interface design, or some other visual or product perspective. As a UX professional you need to focus on what the experience of a product is and how it interacts with the user.

This means being able to determine how an experience happens between a user and a UI in every aspect; what Hardware are they using, what software are they interacting with, what is the way they prefer to search or save material, what problems do they have at work, what problems are they trying to resolve with this product or service. That's what you need to be concerned with. Nobody else is going to care about asking the questions about how the users use the product or service, what their pain points are, or what improvements they would like to see. You are the person that needs to ask this. Even if you don't have access to users, or if you're bringing a new product or service to market and you don't even have users yet, this is where you would create provisional personas.

With provisional personas at least let you get down in writing your understanding of who the different user roles and user groups are going to be with your service or product. This way product, development, UX, business analysis, and the whole team can at least agree upon what you might all think what embodies your users. The provisional persona typically has four parts: facts, problems, needs/goals, and behaviors Those four are where you need to start.

#12: A COMMITTEE CAN GO MARRY THEMSELVES!

One of the most horrible things you're going to encounter, and one of the good behaviors that a UXer will have to adopt, is how you work with design by committee. Basically, when you let design by committee delegate what you do with your work, and they are not experts, you are 100% dooming yourself to absolute and total failure. I know. I know it wasn't your fault, and I completely agree with you. But, even if it isn't your fault, you will be blamed for the failure.

One of the things you have to do is develop the habit of pushing back when you know something isn't right or needs to be changed. It's 100% okay to say that you are an expert when being part of these conversations and kickoffs, and to remind them that you were invited here for your professional perspective and insight. I will tell you right now that this will be a continually challenging area for you, and any other UX professional.

Depending on your background and family, how you argue may be different, but generally speaking a lot of people don't like to argue and they may find this a challenging area. You need to work to improve at negotiating, not arguing, because arguing will always be perceived as a negative, even though the committee is putting you in this situation from the get-go.

I'm warning you now, that there is a potential coming sh*tstorm when you are the lowest rung on the ladder in a committee, and you will be the first to be thrown under the bus when something goes wrong. The best thing to do is document these processes and take notes, and if you have to waste time showing why a committee's suggestions are incorrect, then you have something to prove it with.

What comes to mind, and always in a committee seems to rise to the top of the crap, is 'above the fold', or everything needs to be on screen all at the same time as if people don't scroll ever. It's already a well-established user interaction model that Google researched for years that people start scrolling before an entire screen loads, but there's always going to be some Karen in a committee who is basically going to say everything needs to be on the screen, otherwise "How will users know?"

You will have to demonstrate how users will know and make Karen happy, and you should communicate and document that the reason why the deliverable wasn't done when you wanted was because Karen said we had to go down a rabbit hole to prove my recommendation, because she didn't believe me. That will shut Karen up in future meetings.

#13: RESEARCH AND TIME MANAGEMENT AFTER MARRIAGE.

Let's say you've arrived. You've become a senior UX designer, and you have the title and the pay that you want. But you seem to be wasting a lot of your time on stupid requests, or requests that seem reasonable, but once you look under the hood you see that there's no merit to them.

A habit that you need to form is not letting other people hijack your schedule or waste your time. This will happen specifically with research, because planning and conducting research is very time-consuming. It is 100% likely that you're going to be asked to conduct research and waste time on valueless research, but the truth is there will be no near-term action item or deliverable that needs to occur.

A habit that you may want to start forming and acting on is asking people what the timeline is for executing on these findings, and if they don't have an answer, aren't depending on the research findings, and don't know how it will be included into the roadmap, then it's not important. In this instance you need to communicate that their request will have a lower priority, because there's not really a timeline and it doesn't really affect the road map.

The man behind the curtain in this situation, so to speak, is that you are wasting time with people or teams that have already made up their minds, but they have a checkbox that they have to check called "User Experience." It's required in their process, and so that's why they reached out to you, but they don't really care what you're going to tell them, because they're not going to act on it anyways.

So, the red flag here is when you're asked to perform research, design work, or anything else and you don't get a timeline or an answer to how your work and deliverables affect the product or service. That's when you know that you're wasting your time for projects or services that have already made up their mind, and any UX work that you're doing is just a formality.

It's 100% okay to ask these questions and to tell people that their priority is lower, because there are many other places that will need your help and assistance as a UX professional.

#14: MARRY A DEVELOPER, AND YOU WILL BE HAPPY!

You need to find developers that you can work with and who will champion UX. A lot of people that UXers will encounter, especially in the software development life cycle (but this could also be true for service design) believe that there is value in keeping functionality conversations separate from aesthetic conversations. They are 100% wrong, and I could write an entire book explaining to you why they are 100% wrong.

Just know that thinking that wireframing is a questionable exercise because we could just build it in the code is the answer that you will get, and this directly leads to the fact that 90% of enterprise software is horrible, unusable, and everybody hates it. It's because developers just decided unilaterally if something could be a modal or a drop-down, or how a micro interaction should work. They did what was easy, because as a mechanic they were implementing at a basic level a simple solution. They're not really concerned whether the solution is usable or not.

Now don't get me wrong; you will need to work with developers, and developers are great people, but left to their own devices, without any aesthetic or usability conversations, they're going to do what's easiest and what meets the requirements the quickest. This is not the way. You need to get the developer to spend time with you to work on whiteboarding solutions. This will be frowned upon, because de-velopers are supposed to be chained to a computer like a dog to a dog house and they're supposed to maximize all of their coding and working time. This perspective of chaining a developer to a computer is antiquated and it's just like the metaphor of throwing more developers on a fire to put out the fire.

You need to be able to work smarter not harder, and to do that you need to partner with developers who want to white board with you to come up with how you could develop a user interface interaction that meets requirements, actually works, and can be built in code. This is not a waste of time; this is the best scenario; because this is where you can spend time without a wasting it.

#15: WE MARRIED THE USERS FOR A REASON!

You're going to, at some point, come across user research, either by the result of your own testing in conducting research, or because pre-existing research was handed over to you, and It's going to be tempting to say that users want this or that as an excuse for "I, the UXer," want this. What this always means is that you're jumping to solutions before you have time to wade through the data.

Maybe there's some product people or developers on your team who have heard once or twice, or maybe even heard over and over, that this is what users want. So that's for some reason lodged in their brains that we need to do the certain thing because users want this certain thing. However, doing that certain thing may create a whole new set of problems.

The complex truth of User Experience as a field is this; when you change something here on the left, then it's going to affect something else on the right. It's almost like the butterfly effect, but not bullsh*t. If we start by adding a micro interaction that's exactly like other micro interactions for a new feature, then users most likely can acclimate and use it. However, if we add a new micro interaction or a new design pattern that has never been seen before, when a user starts to interact with it it'll be something new and they may think it works a different way, or they may not entirely understand it.

As a User Experience professional you will need to make decisions based on what research actually says versus what research actually means. There's a great saying in UX that goes, "Everyone wants to innovate, but nobody wants to change." This is 100% true. People will only want to implement or do what they think is easiest, takes the least amount of time, or they think will solve all the problems that they currently have.

The truth is that no problems are solved that easily. Conducting user research and using user data can point you in some helpful directions, but ultimately, you're going to have to try to choose a direction to go with and implement in a way that is not awkwardly juxtaposed with the current service or product. Then you're going to have to retest to see if people understand how to use that. UX is an ongoing process it, doesn't just happen once.

#16: WHY DID YOU TAKE SO LONG TO GET MARRIED?

A good habit to form as a UX professional is not to squander all your time with designs and wireframes. It is very inefficient to spend all your time at the beginning of a project wireframing and designing solutions when you know absolutely f**k all about the problem. You can spend a bunch of time sketching up ideas, wireframing, making style tiles, choosing fonts, and you have done nothing to address the complex usability issues for a new product or service or redesign product or service.

As I said before and I'll say a hundred times over, if you particularly like spending time dabbling with fonts, colors, designs, and how things look, that's great, but you're a UI designer or graphic designer, not a UXer. A UX professional would never start with wire frames. They would start with understanding the asks and the deliverables, and the requirements, understanding the parameters of the project, what are the form factors, what are the operating systems or browsers in which this needs to function, or what are the parameters of the service, the space, and the people who are involved in the service.

Once you have that information, then you can start to do low-fidelity whiteboarding or wireframing, and I wouldn't do that off on your own either. I would do that with other people, hopefully developers as well as product managers. Do not waste time in graphic land with fonts and colors and wireframes, because that's not what's needed from a UX professional.

Form the habit now of getting the information you need to inform the wireframes, otherwise you're just going to be looking at a blank screen on Axure or Adobe XD, and you're just wondering, "What do I make? What needs to go here? And why don't I understand what I need to do?" And you'll just be spinning your wheels. Don't be that person.

#17: YOU HAVE TO MARRY DESIGN!

For all the design bashing that I do, you will have to perform design at some point as a UX professional. I will caution you not to worry about the tools you use, but more so you need to worry about the basics of design. What I mean is the design 101 things that every designer should understand, which basically comes from a course that you took in college about the elements and principles of design.

What I'm talking about is basic color theory; line, shape, color, form, texture, value, and space. These are the visual elements of design. If you are not familiar with what I'm telling you right now, and this all sounds foreign, you don't understand basic design, which is comprised of these elements and principles of design, as well as some Gestalt psychology. You need to stop what you're doing right now, and you need to go learn it. It doesn't matter if you're using the cool newest tool, or if you're using something antiquated like PowerPoint to create designs or mock-ups. That doesn't really matter and nobody on your team for the product or service your building is going to care.

What will be obvious is that you don't understand variety, dominance, harmony, how to use space, how to group similar elements things of that nature which are basic knowledge. It's okay if you don't starting out, because people in UX come from a variety of different backgrounds and fields. Some come from psychology or research, or even statistics, and if you come from one of those disciplines into UX, then you probably don't know design 101.

A lot of designers take for granted the knowledge they have learned, but for others who don't have this knowledge at all it's a deficiency that you need to address. I would highly recommend *Varieties of Visual Experience* by Edmund Burke Feldman, taking a free online design course, or even just studying a little bit about specific things like color theory or Gestalt psychology. This is basic rudimentary design stuff that you need to know, and if you don't know it you need to teach yourself immediately.

#18: MEET THE USERS BEFORE MARRYING THEM!

A good habit to form over your UX career is not to make pixel perfect designs before involving any users. This is a mistake. This is a junior-level mistake. This is almost an unforgivable mistake.

The reason why I tell you this is because you are spending all of your time crafting a perfectly designed solution that's beautiful, has iconography, a style guide, and branding. It looks fantastic but then when you put that in front of a user, you are soon to find out that it doesn't do anything it needs to do, they are not sure how to get the information they need, and it doesn't meet their requirements.

This is why people do low-fidelity design or even paper prototyping. It's important to get something in front of users as soon as soon as possible. It doesn't matter if it's high-fidelity, and it doesn't need to look polished. If you have product sales or business people who tell you otherwise they're wrong. They subscribe to that whole 1960s New York, *Mad Men* razzle-dazzle the client, throw hookers through the window at them and get them drunk approach; and that's just the most bullsh*t way to approach working with clients.

Working with clients and stakeholders should be transparent, it should be collaborative, and it should not be this thing to where we have to impress them. You will waste a lot of time or, worse, take irresponsible or reckless risks that you're just going to have to undo later, which will then compound and take even more time to fix the problems. You need to be able to work very quickly and responsively in agile, and to do that you need to work very lo-fidelity. You need users sooner rather than later. You can't spend six months working on a project and then put it in front of a user and wonder why it didn't work, it was broken, or they had a bad reaction to the design. You could have, in a week, put something low-fidelity in front of users and got more valuable information and feedback.

This is *Lean UX*, and if you don't know what *Lean UX* is please get the book about it, because *Lean UX* is a proven technique born out of Toyota's manufacturing model. *Lean UX* speaks to finding information out as you go from users as opposed to doing this 'waterfall thing' where you're waiting till the end, and trying to get buy in from users you've never validated your product against.

Work low-fidelity, work with users as soon as possible, and adjust accordingly; it will be quicker and easier to do than the alternative.

#19: I MARRIED A DESIGNER, NOT A DESIGN THINKER!

A good thing to understand and a good habit to form in order to avoid wasting time unlearning tools and software is to ignore whatever the new hotness is in design. There's always going to be design fads; people will run over to Material icons, and then back over to FontAwesome, and then back over to Android's icons, and so on, because they are the new big thing.

So instead of wasting time learning the new hotness, you should probably spend more time learning how to think like a designer. There's a whole field of study called Design Management and that field specifically trains you to think like a designer, not to create art, design, and mock-ups for UI like a designer. Design Management as a field is putting you in the position of becoming a design thinking person, which is foremost someone who can facilitate creative thinking. It's more productive for you to facilitate design thinking than to just create beautifully designed solutions.

You will find out that creating designs and colors and styles is easy. It's easy work that anyone can do. It's so easy, that there are computer programs that do it. It's so easy that you can go and buy any template for a Squarespace site or a WordPress site because there are so many designers out there in the field, and the field is completely oversaturated. So, don't worry about design, worry about design thinking and facilitating design thinking. If you're not sure what design thinking is please go immediately out and search for it on the web.

Basically, what you need to be able do is have a group of diverse people who are developers, product people, stakeholders, clients, business analysts, and so on, that you can run through activities with design in mind. This will have benefits to the project kind of like what a product manager ought to provide, but they don't have the skill set for it, most of the time. Most of the product people that you're going to run into are only going to be a communication bottleneck between the client, the stakeholders, and the team, or they just know how to make JIRA tickets and run sprints and reviews.

Facilitating design thinking is a skill that your team needs, and if your product people cannot do this, you will need to be able to do it. You will need to be able to run sessions on how to create objectives and key results (OKRs), or how to plan with service mapping or service blueprinting how an existing product works for redesign. These will be assets and tools that people will use in your project, and no one's going to make them, or know how to make them, except you: the UX professional.

So, step away from the fonts, the icons, and the colors, and maybe step towards how you can facilitate design thinking, mapping, and research

#20: SHOULD I MARRY FOR QUANTITY OR QUALITY?

Another good habit to form is understanding the difference between qualitative and quantitative research. It's also good to learn when to use one versus the other.

For example; quantitative analysis without talking to users is going to better capture what the users are actually saying rather than what they're actually doing. On the other hand, you need to consider that quantitative data is that it's largely self-reported. For example: let's say you have an eCommerce website where you're selling something, and the quantitative data that you are getting is user reports through that eCommerce website. Well, you should know that 90% of what you get are going to be complaints or problems that users have with the system. It's going to be very unlikely that people are going to tell you that they had a great experience, because people generally just expect things to work correctly (I know crazy right?). The other 10% may say all they had a great experience, but you may never ever get to hear that.

So, you should understand that when delivering insights to change the user interface for a service or product that you're going to get different types of information from qualitative versus quantitative data. The *Nielsen Norman Group* suggest that you really only need 5 people when conducting a usability test, which is a qualitative source of data. On the other hand, if you're looking for confirmation and you're wanting to know answers that are quantifiable like a system usability scale (SUS), or you're just trying to confirm understanding of a metric, that is quantitative data which can be administered through a survey of no more than 250 people.

So, don't cross the two, I guess is what I'm telling you. You need to be able to understand the difference between them and the value of each, and don't interpose the two because it will lead to problems with your user's experience.

20 Ways to Kill Your Career

#1: THIS WOULD BE KILLER IF IT WAS INTERACTIVE!

Working in UX one of the things that people want are prototypes, wireframes, comps, or whatever terms are interchangeable for that. I've written a lot on this subject

The terminology is very different from person to person, and project to project. I prefer to think of prototypes as a trifecta in which the parts of that trifecta are fidelity, operability, and interactivity.

- **Fidelity** refers to the degree of accuracy and quality with which the user interface is produced.
- **Interactivity** is the ability to interact with a human user to obtain and give information.
- **Operability** is the data and technology capability of being put into use, operation, or practice.

So, people now expect interactivity at a higher fidelity, and I'm starting to see more people wanting operability, meaning that they want dynamic data pulling into it. Unfortunately, operability – where you are pushing and pulling data into a prototype – it's something that's not easily accomplished without a developer, but a higher-fidelity and interactivity is something that is possible.

More and more I see the desire for interactive prototypes and so that's something that we just have to do as UXers now. So, if you don't want to fail, get some interactivity, in any way possible, into your prototypes. Try to think of the possibilities of how interaction could work or, if you're redesigning, how interaction failed in past experience. By including interactivity at an early stage, it allows you to have say in the interaction design, which you should, as opposed to not having a seat at all and letting development build whatever is easiest.

#2: WILL FAILURE KILL ME?

First and foremost, you should never believe in failure. It's like the saying goes, "Fail fast and fail often... but don't actually put power or energy into failure."

You must start to look at work that you do in UX as either learning something, or not learning something. Both are valuable lessons, and despite project success, you will have learned something valuable or learned something not to do. The one thing that's true about lessons in UX is also the same thing that's true about history, and that's that lessons are repeated until they are learned.

You will encounter a lot of different teams as a UX professional wherein you will be working towards a product or service goal, and if things are not going ideally or there isn't clarity on the project or deliverables, it's easy to give in to the fact that the project's going to fail, everything you're going to do is going to fail, and failure should never be an option.

This is the wrong mentality to have. What you need to learn is that not believing in failure will let you focus on what it is you need to do, what it is you need to deliver, and when you need to deliver it. Yes, it may be the case that a project is so screwed up that you have no idea what to do, and you're just holding and waiting, but that's not your fault. Take action on what you can take action on, and work smarter not harder.

#3: THIS IS WHY WE KILL TO TALK TO THE USER!

One thing you can do to immediately fail as a UXer is not advocate, include, or even listen to your user. UX as a discipline fails when you don't continuously push for the voice of the user and make usability a part of every conversation in the product or service design lifecycle.

The majority of the time, as you tackle different projects throughout your career, no one is going to advocate for the user except for you. Yes, you will encounter some product people who have some UX skills and interests, but at the end of the day the product is their focus and not the user. What your being paid for is to advocate for the user data, not the user, but rather the user data. We can't do everything that the users want, but we can analyze and advocate for user data as a way to talk and interact with our users, and for ways to test our products and services against user expectations.

This type of advocacy for the UX process is something you simply must do 100% of the time. You will fail if you do not advocate for understanding the user, interacting with users, using and utilizing user data, or testing products and services with users. You're a UX professional; that is your job!

#4: WHO DO I HAVE TO KILL TO CHAMPION UX?

Let's face it you're going to have frustrations. UX will be an uphill battle at most places you'll work. If you want to lessen your frustration, and not fail right out of the gate, you need to understand that part of your position and your responsibility is going to be teaching and increasing others' awareness of UX practices and your general design ability.

This doesn't mean that you need to teach people Design 101 or User Experience 101, but it does mean that you may have to talk about color theory to a developer. You may need to talk about or educate a product person on bias and usability testing. You may have to talk to a business analyst about how empathy mapping can get you better JIRA tickets. This is part of your job, unfortunately, because UX as a field is still growing, and awareness of best practices is still absent.

So, embrace the fact that you need to educate, and that you're going to have to constantly inform others about UX practices, and you will do fine.

#5: KILLING HEURISTIC BIASES

Something else that can lead to failure for companies in general, as well as growing UX teams, is that it's important to hire complementary people rather than similar people in the name of fitting a culture.

If you hire every good designer to outfit your UX team, you're soon going to realize that you don't have anyone with strengths in facilitating design thinking, or doing/conducting design research. The same goes when you're doing a kickoff meeting, and in that you have 15 Developers and one UX professional. New and diverse points of view are crucial when working collaboratively across disciplines like development, product, sales, and design.

This is not just for hiring, but this is also for how you work. You do not want to be the UX professional who is not talking to or working with anyone else, and off designing in a bubble. You need different voices at the table when you design a user interface from requirements, when you conduct user testing, and when you write usability study scripts. It seems obvious that there's more value when team members are complementary to each other, however, I've worked for many companies and organizations who have only hired the same type of people at every single interview.

I remember one time I was asked to attend an interview where the person could juggle and they spoke three languages, but they're code skills were maybe not up to par but at a basic web designer level. I thought that all of their other skill sets and experience would be invaluable for our team, but I was voted down by a majority because everyone else was looking for the same type of person... a junior web designer focused solely was on design, HTML, and CSS.

When I tried to make a case as to why this other person's varied experience and perspectives would add to our team instead of the same kind of person we already had working for us, it fell on deaf ears. It's at that point I realized that the team on which I was working wasn't very diverse, and we were just kind of a gray pudding with the same heuristic biases.

#6: YOU NEED TO KILL YOUR EGO!

One of the fastest ways to fail in UX is not listening to others and letting your ego wedge its way into your work and workplace relationships. Your ego can kill you! If you can't be wrong, you can't be in the field.

I am constantly amazed by all the times that I have performed an initial UX audit of an enterprise web application, predicted what the usability errors were and how to improve them, and then wrote a test along the lines of testing for that specific usability error… only to find out that I was completely shocked and surprised by the outcomes and findings of the usability test.

This is the one thing I can definitely say about usability testing: you will always be surprised by the test results that you get. UX is all about community value and not being of a singular mind. It can be hard to pour work into something and watch it fail, but honestly it happens all the time. Yes, you can view this as a learning experience, but UXers should also learn to step back, listen, let go of your ego, and give yourself over to truly understanding usability problems.

Having this open perspective when you listen will help improve your research, which in turn helps improve your design solutions. At the end of the day, you want your professional reputation and your UX methodology to be reflected in the improvements you make and how you work with other team members, and not as a reflection on you as a person.

#7: YOU MUST LEARN TO GO FOR THE KILL!

A quick way to fail, assuredly, in the field of UX is not fighting for your conclusions. You have to be seen as a valuable member of your product or service team and not that person that throws a report down and says, "These are our findings, do whatever you want with it."

I learned a long time ago working in corporate eCommerce as a designer on their UX team that you never just hand over the usability report, the user data, or the findings. Never, ever do this! You want to actually schedule a meeting with your team, stakeholder, product person, or whomever you are delivering your UX research and testing reports to. You need the opportunity to walk them through it, explain your process, create transparency, and explain why you recommend the solutions that you have recommended from user data insights.

Doing this will get people on your side more than just making a pretty report and handing it out will. People appreciate follow through. It's easy for mid-level UX professionals to come to the conclusion that, "Hey, we can put together the best insights and the best recommendations, but they'll just do what they want. This is incorrect, and it is not the way you should look at UX. You're just one Cog in the machine that is concerned about the product. So by tempering your reports with an understanding of what the business requirements, deadlines, and deliverables are be for clients, as well as communicating once you've completed the research and recommendations to the appropriate people, you will be more aware of the situation and you will have more weight at the table to influence decisions.

#8: I WOULD KILL TO UNDERSTAND THE BUSINESS GOALS!

It's easy to be blissfully and blithely unaware of the business goals of the company in which you are employed, and it's also one of the easiest and fastest ways to fail as a UXer. If you don't know how you plug in to the services and products that your company is building or redesigning, and you don't understand what success looks like for the business, what the OKRs (objective and key results) are for that product or service, or even what a KPI (key performance indicator) is for that product then what the f**k are you doing?

Remember that you're getting a paycheck every two weeks from this company. Yes, your title may be "something User Experience something," but technically you're still working for a business organization that has a product or service to distribute, sell, improve, redesign, etc. You cannot walk around touting your UX puritanism, because you are the only person who has the user in mind, and you want to do what's best for the user, and if only everyone would listen to you then you would have a better product!

These trappings and delusions of grandeur are just not true, and they're indicative of someone who thinks like a very inexperienced UXer. You need to be aware of your business' goals, and then you are in a better place to see how you can align user goals to business goals. That's the win-win scenario.

You can act like a UX paladin in shining armor – that does nothing but phenomenal work and makes phenomenal suggestions for the user – but at the end of the day that's really not what's needed. What's needed is someone to work with the team to improve the product or service, and you can't do that if you're not aware of business goals.

#9: KILL YOURSELF IF YOU THINK YOU'RE THE USER!

You are not the user. The developer is not the user. The product manager, or product owner is not the user. The client is not the user.

This may sound like common sense, but you will be surprised how many times this actually comes up in your career. One of the fastest ways to fail is treating stakeholders, sales reps, developers, product people, or even treating yourself, as the user.

Once you go down this road it's a slippery slope. You start to make decisions on behalf of the user, you start to have preferences on the behalf of the user. You start to jump to assumptions and conclusions about how the user would do something. And so, on and so forth… it never ends. Where you will find yourself is releasing a product or service that doesn't align with user expectations, and you will ask yourself how did we get here? It's because of you, you dumbf**k! It's because you, as a UX professional, didn't stand up and say, "We're not the users! We need to actually talk to some users."

And you know what, we're probably not going to get them for free. We're probably going to have to pay users, or incentivize them in some way to give us free work, through usability tests, focus groups, and other forms of usability research. It's a hard pill to swallow but once you do swallow it, everything will be better.

#10: The PM Killed Me With What They Said!

People who go into the UX field will have to have tough skin. One of the quickest ways to fail is not being able to receive constructive criticism, harsh feedback, or other ammunition from the slings and arrows that are going to be fired at you. Everyone's highly critical of UX, and since you have your finger in many pies, like research, design, some front-end development, business goals, etc. you're going to get a lot of healthy criticism and skepticism from other people on your team, business, or organization.

This is fine. This is normal. People who come from a design or art background are very much used to this. Sitting through collegiate level critiques is one of the most grueling and painful things that your ego must undergo. However, those people who can come out the other end develop tough skin and learn how to separate the vitriol from the value. You will need to learn how to do this if you don't want to fail.

You need to actually find an equilibrium between visual design and functional usability. You need to find an equilibrium between user goals and business goals. The only way to do this is to listen to the technology concerns of your development team, listen to the product team's perspective on the road map, deliverables, and deadlines, and to work within those constraints, and try not to get butt hurt about it.

At the end of the day it's a job, and you're getting paid for this job, so provide your professional perspective and opinion. Make your suggestions, do your work, and just realize that there will be conflict at work and you will still have to come in the next day regardless. Checking your ego at the door is a good thing, and I would highly advise, again, that you adopt a perspective of no attitude and no ownership.

#11: I WOULD KILL TO UNDERSTAND THIS DATA!

If don't want to fail hard and \fast, and trash your career while you're doing it, you need to understand what you're doing. This goes back to the fake it until you make it thing, but more specifically for UX, if you don't know what you're doing, and you just go online to identify a medium length article that gives you suggestions, and you implement that and it's not really the data that you need and you can't really make sense out of it… who's to blame?

You need to be able to understand data. You need to be able to understand clicks, throughputs, and the conversion funnel, or whatever your company uses to measure success with key performance indicators (KPIs). You need to be able to set up your testing in such a way, by writing usability scripts or screening of users, to get the data that you specifically need to answer questions. If you want to fail, then you can bring in irrelevant information that has no bearing on the problem that you're trying to solve. People will see this, people will know it's bullsh*t, and people will call you on your bullsh*t.

If you don't have a great technique to prioritize, sort, and visualize data, that's fine, but try something that actually makes sense and communicate that with transparency to your team.

A great example of this is the feature matrix. A lot of people don't know where to start when they do competitive benchmarking, but a feature matrix is someplace to say, "Well we can at least look at these other services or products that are similar. They do this…" Count the number of other companies doing what they do, and if at least

60% to 75% of your peers are doing it, and you're not, that probably means you're deficient.

In the end you can always fall back on percentages and numbers, but you need to make Excel your friend, you need to understand data, and you need to be able to communicate what data means to members of your team and the business at large. If you cannot do this, or you're unwilling, then that means you're accepting failure.

You can't do UX without talking to the user, which involves getting user data from research, and that's going to involve math and numbers. Suck it up UXer, and do the work.

#12: I WOULD KILL FOR USERS!

One of the fastest ways to fail is to be slow to get users involved with designing, or redesigning, your product or service.

One of the principles of Lean UX is getting users involved as soon as possible and having them continually involved in the lean sprint cycle. Even if you're just at the beginning, you're not sure of all the technical details yet, and you're just creating UI wireframes to get requirements down in some whiteboard sketches, try to get those in front of users if you can. Whiteboard sketching is essentially paper prototyping.

20 years into the 21st century tools like Balsamiq are great because it lets you create something quickly, especially if you can't draw. if you can draw, do that first; it'll always be quicker to whiteboard or sketch something on paper than to use a graphic user interface and a software (that probably requires a subscription) just to build your first wireframes.

If you're not near your users, do a screen share remotely. There are tons of free software that do this. Send them images or, even better, a low-fidelity interactive prototype and watch the user, ask them questions over the phone while they are using it, and don't forget to play reporter. By playing reporter, I mean delve deeper and deeper like an actual reporter would do, and ask why a user did a certain thing or if they say "I would expect this to be in the top left" ask them why they would expect it to be in the top left.

Then, as much as you can through sprint cycles, try to stay a sprint ahead of development so you can have user interfaces and tests against users, before developers are working on the actual wireframes.

Engage users as soon as possible, use them often, and use them as much as possible.

#13: WILL WE GET KILLED IF WE AREN'T ACCESSIBLE?

If you want to fail, and fail hard, not factoring accessibility into your digital projects and products is the way to go. We are now in a post WCAG 2.0 society, and people commonly know in software development what AA and AAA accessibility standards are. If not, you should be concerned about their level of expertise.

There are tools now like Axe, WAVE, JAWS that let developers start to tackle with and resolve accessibility problems sooner, rather than later. Don't get me wrong this is a good thing, but how does that affect the UX professional? What you need to do, is to get your accessibility check in the first days of an audit or a redesign. Do not wait for users to complain or for your company or organization to be sued, because then it will be too late.

There are tools out there with accessibility inspectors and editors, but there are also color contrast tools and dedicated server-side software, like SiteImprove or ComplianceSheriff, that you can use to meet these standards.

I'm going to tell you that, when you're out there in the workforce, you're not going to work on a digital project that has an accessibility team. I've never encountered one in 10 plus years. Accessibility has kind of fallen under User Experience so start incorporating it into your process and be ready to answer how you would fix accessibility errors.

#14: I WOULD KILL FOR DIRECTION!

Never fail to ask the tough questions. In addition to that, never fail to ask the questions you should when you're onboarded into a new product or team. Many times, I have started a new project as a consultant, as a contractor, or subcontractor and no one even bothered to introduce me, let alone introduce the reason why we were designing the product.

I often find that a lot of the first steps in starting a project, redesign, or trying to bring something new to market, get overlooked. I have specific steps that I follow when I'm in this situation. I have to ask the tough questions and you are going to have to do the same. I need to get on the same page as the rest of the team, I need to understand what the OKRs are, I need to know what the KPIs are, and I need to know what the customer lifecycle is. If I don't know what our goals are, what success looks like, and how we are selling our product or service, then how can I do my job?

The 100% truth is that most products fail, and most independent research and development (IRAD) fails. In order to avoid this, you have to ask the tough questions to get directions. Detecting signs that something isn't going right and then responding to that by pushing for the information that you need, is the thing that you need to do to serve users.

User experience is not a comfortable position. You're not going to get instructions and, often times, people are going to look to you for guidance because they have no idea what your area of expertise skill set are So, as a UXer, you need to embrace uncertainty, a lack of knowledge about your profession, and you may need to ask the tough questions to inform the team on how to move forward.

#15: JUST KILL ME NOW, BECAUSE WE DIDN'T PLAN FOR THAT!

One of the first things I do when I start working on a product, project, or service is having conversations with a lot of people. I talk to project managers and, potentially, users and business analysts to find out what the requirements are. This is mainly due to the one of the biggest questions that I'm going to have in my head, which is, "Who are the users and what are the user roles?"

I want to know if, for example, when you're designing a digital application for a hospital's post-acute care, who are all the different users? Let's say there's a counselor, a nurse, a nurse manager, and a nurse director. That would be good to know, because in an agile software development life cycle, and when working in a start-up atmosphere, you need to be able to shift rapidly and work efficiently. For a UXer, what that means is that you are going to probably spend the majority of your time designing complex enterprise software applications from a super admin perspective.

It's easier to disable features or turn things off for different user roles and permissions. I need to know though, beforehand, what are the types of users that we are trying to work for? To me this is not trying to fabricate personas that don't have any value, this is actually the exact opposite. For me this is how we start to build provisional personas. And then we can start to understand the world, the role, the service, and the function of the project we're designing.

I have to be able to put my mind into that of different users, and as a UXer I need to create and understand the relevant real-world constraints that the different types of users will be facing. So even though personas could be perceived as a waste of time, I would highly advise that, in order not to fail, at bare minimum flush out what the user roles are so you know beforehand when you're designing.

It's harder to change down the road, and one of my favorite metaphors that a colleague shared with me years ago is that we, "can't unbake the cake." We can change the frosting and we can put stuff on the outside, but with the core cake we can't go back and put in a different ingredient. The same thing goes for UX and users.

#16: MY IDEAS ARE KILLER!

One of the fastest ways to fail in User Experience is to be close-minded. It's that simple. This could happen to you so be warned. It's easy to get halfway down the road and have so many projects go bad over time that you become jaded. Your work becomes lackluster because you don't see how usability is going to improve for projects going forward. You become that angry person in meetings that people don't like. You become that person who's short with everybody. And you just start to use your own ideas and not listen to anyone else.

You may be searching for that special project or product where you can hope to get everything right, and if people would just listen to you and let you do what you know to do, it'll be perfect. I'm here to tell you that no product is perfect, everything can be improved, and usability is something that's constantly changing due to new features being added to products.

Instead of being close minded and thinking that only your ideas are correct, maybe you should be focusing on getting inspiration from outside of your field, talking, being collaborative, and communicating with other professionals. If you're in a rut and you're getting a little jaded, you need to start looking at other user interfaces. I would highly recommend that you start to look at other interactive media like video games, or tabletop board games, or even data visualization.

All of these will have new ways to interact with and view data, and it's good to have different experiences with UX outside of the workplace. Some of the best ideas that I've had for enterprise software applications have come from a video game that I was playing, or a board game that I played when I got together with a group of friends.

Don't be afraid to stay open-minded, and if you find yourself moving toward being close-minded, stop, and start doing fun things with other people. This way you'll be open to inspiration from a multitude of different areas and ideas that come from a multitude of different people. Who knows they, could have a better idea than you had.

#17: I'm gagging... This trend is killer!

One of the exciting things about working in UX, and about being a professional in the field, is that things are constantly changing. There's always going to be new designs, there's always going to be better, more improved websites, there's going to be better software applications, there's going to be cooler video games, and there's going to be cooler user interfaces.

There will be new trends that pop up every year about how to show information, how to design things, and how to change micro interactions. UX is hot right now, and it's a bustling and growing field. However, I will caution you to stick to what works in research as opposed to just following trends. I probably don't have to tell you this, but following trends really gets you nothing more than being trendy.

Users understand how to scroll, users understand that underlined blue text on the internet is clickable. People understand what accordions are, and how drop down and slide out menus work. As the whole digital ecosphere moves along, users move with it and they expect new micro interactions that really work that are easy and which they understand to be universal. Unfortunately, that's just the way the evolution of UX works in tandem with user expectations.

So, I'm not saying not to follow the trends, or that you'll fail if you do, but rather what I'm saying is definitely look at a trend... follow it, do some research, and, if it's successful and you have improved metrics like reduced task completion time, reduced error rates, and an increase in success rates, then definitely Incorporate it.

I'm just cautioning you not to follow a trend for the purpose of following a trend when it actually could be decreasing the usability of your product or service.

#18: I WOULD KILL TO BE IN THAT MEETING!

I will caution you at this point that instead of failing that you should do the exact opposite. You should succeed! You should be at the table with the decisions being made on a product. You should want to be in those meetings. You should ask to attend product meetings; you should ask in what other ways how you can be involved and what you can do to help the team.

If you want to help groom a backlog of JIRA tickets do so, if you want to learn more about product work and you want input on writing user stories then do so. Be present and be mindful, and you won't fail.

You need to make yourself valuable, and you need the team to see that so that they will engage you and involve you in the decision-making process. By not adding value and just going back to your cubicle and working on your design, you are just a deliverable in a JIRA ticket that has time going to it... and you are just a checkbox that needs to be checked.

Don't be that type of UXer, but rather engage your team and show your value... dive right in!

#19: You Have to Kill for the User Data!

A challenge you're going to face in the UX profession is difficult users. If your users are active duty soldiers and are on base, or they are nurse managers who don't have a lot of time off, or they are hospital administrators… you're not going to have a bunch of time to work with them. Not mention your own availability and the limited resources in a budget.

In these instances, in order not to fail, you need to take usability testing to them. If you didn't already know, usability testing is a way to get data about how people use designs and this data is used to make decisions to improve a website, web app, gadget, service, or product. Usability testing is a major tool of the UX professional, and usually this involves recording the user interacting with your product… recording their audio, what they are doing on the screen, and maybe even their facial expressions.

However, often times, in these situations you are going to have to travel to your user's specific location and perform usability testing. In addition to that, this type of bootleg or guerrilla usability testing is going to require you to conduct it within a time crunch, and in an uncertain environment where you don't know if you will have internet or a projector. So, it's important for you not to fail, but also for you to be very adaptable and change things on the fly, and work around technical problems.

A great solution for this is developing a mobile usability testing lab. A mobile usability testing lab has the basics that you need to conduct a usability test, and it can be set up in your office, but it can be packed up and moved at a moment's notice to conduct testing in the field. All you need is some type of recording software, a laptop with a webcam, and something to carry it all in. You can go with very low-cost solutions to make it easy and budget light, or it could be the exact opposite and be budget intensive, and, in that case, really pay for software suites, quality microphones and cameras. How not to fail is having adaptability and versatility in testing, and this is going to be important to you in the long run.

#20: How the F**k Do We Get Data?

A problem I run into a lot with UXers is data mining and the usage of analytical data. For you as a UX professional, data mining is going to be very useful. The goal here is for you to generate new information from large amounts of data.

Over the years, I've come to understand that everyone's experience with analytical data is different and varies greatly. However, what you need to know is that third-party software applications, simple browser extensions, or dedicated software suites can provide you with valuable data. Some third-party application examples are CrazyEgg, Forsee, and PageFair which are ways to conduct heat mapping, customer intercepts for surveys and questionnaires, and detection of ad blocking software, if you're working with web applications or websites.

When you're considering giant software solutions, Adobe Marketing Cloud and Google Analytics are pretty much the heavy contenders for the analytic circle. For dedicated browser tools, which are free, most browsers have devtools in them like Chrome Dev tools, but there's also browser add-ons for accessibility for detecting fonts and seeing what frameworks are being used.

All in all, you can work with all of these things together to get more and more information about your users, what their behaviors are, their demographics, and what they're doing. There's no excuse for not having data, because, even if you're working on strict government or protected web applications, you can take server-side analytics and this is way more informative than just logs, like access and error logs.

If you do not have data and immediately find a way to get data or set up data tracking, there's a lot of free software out there to do this, and within a short time, in less than four weeks you've already collected a month of data concerning what your users are doing and you'll have something to work with.

Conclusion

I have been working in the field for a very long time, and although sometimes I get frustrated as h*ll as UXer, in the end it's the positive people and projects that rise to the top of the sh*tpile. Jobs come and go, coworkers come and go, and in the end, you will measure the value of your career by the knowledge you've gained, the cool people you meet, and the awesome things you got to do and be part of.

You will always have to pay bills (and f**king taxes), so don't sweat the small stuff in life… likewise, don't sweat the small stuff in your career.

So hopefully this book helps you dodge some of the curve balls that will be thrown at a UXer. Hopefully it gives you some good habits to cultivate, and hopefully you better see the red flags to avoid committing career suicide.

Safe travels UXer :)